C000227251

the
natural
home

household
lore and
remedies
that actually
work

the
natural home

Rosamond Richardson

with photographs by
Michelle Garrett

Kyle Cathie Limited

First published in Great Britain in 2001 by
Kyle Cathie Limited
122 Arlington Road, London NW1 7HP

ISBN 1 85626 416 5

All rights reserved. No reproduction, copy or transmission of this publication
may be made without written permission. No paragraph of this publication
may be reproduced, copied or transmitted save with written permission or in
accordance with the provision of the Copyright Act 1956 (as amended). Any
person who does any unauthorised act in relation to this publication may be
liable to criminal prosecution and civil claims for damages.

Text © 1997, 2001 Rosamond Richardson
Photographs © 1997 Michelle Garrett (except where listed below)
Design by Robert Updegraff

Most of the material in this book is taken from COUNTRY WISDOM by
Rosamond Richardson, published in 1997

Rosamond Richardson is hereby identified as the author of this work in
accordance with Section 77 of the Copyright, Designs and Patents Act 1988

A CIP catalogue record for this title is available from the British Library

Production by Lorraine Baird & Sha Huxtable
Colour reproduction by ChromaGraphics, Singapore
Printed and bound in Italy by Printer Trento S. r. l.

Photography credits: page 6 A-Z Botanical Collection; page 25 House &
Interiors; page 29 Donna Eaves; page 56 Tim Winter (fireplace designed by
Mark Watson); page 60 Jacqui Hurst; page 61 Holt Studio International/Nigel
Cattlin; page 67 Ecoscene/Ian Beames

CONTENTS

INTRODUCTION

Mid pleasures and palaces though we may roam,
Be it ever so humble, there's no place like home.
J.H. Payne, 1791-1852

Whether your home is ever so humble, or a palace, or something in between, it is
your castle. If you live in a city or town you may dream of making your home in the
countryside with its inky starlit nights and fresh air, to feel the changing climate
through the turning seasons, to be subject to the moods of nature to which urban life
is less exposed. Whether your home is a refuge from pollution and noise, or looks out
on to the lanes and fields, looking after it takes a significant amount of time and
energy. We learn some lessons from the experience of our mothers and
grandmothers, the rest we pick up as we go along. There is a rich store of wisdom
from the days before heavy chemicals were used in cleaning and washing; some of it is
just as appropriate to today's world as it was then and can be updated to modern
needs. I have collected tips from people who live or have lived in far-flung corners of
the world – Singapore, Zimbabwe, Brazil, St Helena, China, Holland and Germany as
well as the UK and USA. What is surprising is how many of the practical tips overlap,
even though they originate from unconnected cultures. For example, salt recurs
universally and lemons are ubiquitous.

North American Indians had a tradition of salt being used to overcome bad
energies in the house: sprinkling salt in the corners of each room creates a protective
circle which invites in the Spirit of the Wind. Interestingly, Jews have a custom of

Plants and natural materials help make the kitchen the heart of any house.

7

presenting salt (and bread) to the new owner of a house on their first visit. And there is an English tradition of sprinkling salt in front of the threshold before you take ownership.

There are endless touches that constitute the art of home-making. The use of colour, or the way you arrange the furniture and ornaments, expresses something about who you are. Rudolf Steiner said that 'you never see a straight line in nature, so try imitating the curves of the natural world in your furniture and fittings'. Bringing houseplants into the home increases the healthy ions in the atmosphere; candlelight can transform an occasion, and an open fire gives cosiness and focus to

The aroma of freshly baked bread is one of the most enticing in the home.

Rose petals in homemade pot pourri add a touch of elegance as well as fragrance.

cold winter nights. The family festivals that punctuate the year have as their focus hearth and home, underlining the central importance of the home-making aspect of our family life.

The task of keeping the home fresh and clean is eternal. Using natural as opposed to chemical ingredients makes your house smell good and prevents it being polluted by some of the toxic gases given off by synthetic cleaners. Cheap and easy to use, these materials really do work, the natural way, and are just as handy for computer keys as they were for scouring the pans before the days of stainless steel. You can control household pests, keep the bathroom spotless, remove unwanted cooking smells and remove stains without resorting to an array of chemicals. Try it: it works.

KITCHEN

'A general anarchy prevails in my kitchen,' wrote the lugubrious Dr. Johnson: perhaps he needed a touch of Feng Shui, which prescribes an airy, spacious and well-lit kitchen. Associated with the health of the family, it should be a calm environment with as many natural materials as possible – cane, raffia, wood and clay. Green houseplants deflect bad energy and ionise the atmosphere, although spiky cacti are not auspicious (anything with sharp angles deflects good energy). Keeping the kitchen clean the natural way, without resorting to chemicals, will ensure that it smells good. Friends from all over the world have contributed their tips on how to keep this centre of the home bright and fragrant using ordinary kitchen ingredients.

Dealing with strong smells

To remove strong smells on wooden boards after chopping onions, garlic or fish, rub the area with the cut side of half a lemon. If your hands smell strongly of garlic, rub some English mustard powder into them before washing them – this neutralises the smell. To clean pans in which you have cooked fish, and which still retain the smell, rub well with a cut lemon after washing, then rinse thoroughly.

If the bread bin smells musty, wipe it with a little white vinegar on a damp cloth and leave it open to dry. This will also get rid of any mildew. For smells in the fridge, leave a bowl filled with cat litter, bicarbonate of soda or charcoal: they all absorb smells. If the microwave gets smelly, half-fill a small bowl with water, add 3-4 tablespoons of lemon juice and run on high for 1 minute. Remove the bowl and wipe the oven clean.

If the smell of cigarette smoke lingers, light a candle for half an hour or so to get rid of the smell. To lessen the smell in the first place, put a dish of water mixed with vinegar in a discreet place near to the smoker, and some of the smell will be neutralised.

Lemon and salt are excellent natural cleansers.

Simmering spices in water gives the kitchen a beautiful aroma and disguises any unwanted cooking smells. Try cinnamon with a little brown sugar in water over a very low heat, or simply use several cloves or a sliced up lemon.

Damp cupboards

Fill a coffee can with charcoal briquets, punch holes in the sides and lid, and place it in the cupboard to absorb moisture. Or you can tie pieces of chalk together and hang them inside the cupboard. If you have a damp outside wall, plant sunflowers against it. A Dutch friend who lived on marshlands told me this, and I tried it in a cottage where I used to live. It worked, and the sunflowers gave me a lot of pleasure as I worked in the kitchen.

Cast-iron pans

Cast-iron pans rust easily, and the best technique to prevent this happening is to rub them with vegetable oil after washing, then drying them thoroughly with kitchen paper. If, however, they do rust, rub the area with a solution of 1 tablespoon citric acid in 600 ml/1 pint water, and this will remove it. A Norwegian friend told me that her grandmother boiled pots and pans with horse-droppings to prevent rust....

Aluminium and stainless steel saucepans

A woman in the village who has been doing cleaning work all her life told me that for discoloured pans she boils rhubarb or lemon juice to remove staining. If the bottom gets burnt, fill with cold water and leave for an hour. Then add some borax powder or cream of tartar and boil. The burnt food will come away without injuring the pan.

Alternatively, fill the pan with water and add a sliced onion plus a tablespoon of salt. Boil for 10 minutes, then leave to soak overnight. The residue will wash away easily.

For marks on stainless steel, rub with a handful of flour, then polish with a soft cloth. If it is badly marked, use a scouring pad and lemon juice.

Simmering spices gives the kitchen a beautiful aroma.

Clean copper pans with a cloth soaked in vinegar to maintain this lovely sheen.

Copper

When heavily tarnished, an English country remedy is to rub the coat of grime with crushed rhubarb leaves, or use the cut side of a lemon dipped in fine salt. A Belgian friend suggests filling a plant-spray bottle with vinegar, spray it on and allow to stand for several hours, then rub clean.

If copper turns green, remove the verdigris with a solution of ammonia, using rubber gloves.

Cleaning the oven

Everyone's least favourite task is made easier if you rub the oven clean with a damp cloth dipped in bicarbonate of soda. For heavy soiling, mix 1 tablespoon of paraffin with 2 tablespoons of salt and scrub into the staining. Rinse off with hot water and washing soda (using rubber gloves).

Pouring salt on to food-spills on the stove while you are cooking prevents them burning. This also works inside the oven and is very useful – I am forever having overflows in the oven which burn horribly. This treatment prevents the worst of the smells.

Pot plants

Keeping pot plants in the kitchen and around the house maintains a good ion balance in the atmosphere, and brings life and beauty into a room. Feng Shui recommends replacing dying plants with healthy ones, and removing decaying leaves. All houseplants need loving care, and an occasional ecologically friendly spray to keep pests away.

Indoor plant insecticide

> *a handful of pipe or cigarette tobacco*
> *450ml (¾ pint) water, heated*
> *4 teaspoons washing-up liquid*

Pour hot water over the tobacco in a bowl and leave overnight. Strain off. Add to the liquid soap and mix well. Pour into a plant-spray bottle and spray the leaves on both sides.

A little oil of citronella placed near to plants will also repel insects and scent the kitchen pleasantly.

I find that indoor plants flourish if watered with the rinsings of the milk bottle three times a week. Arrange small pebbles on top of the earth around pot plants to keep the moisture in. If you have hanging plants, use cracked nutshells collected at Christmas as lightweight drainage material so that there is less strain on the wall and on the basket handle.

Washing up

For those eternal tea stains on mugs, dip a damp cloth into bicarbonate of soda and rub the stain off. This also works for cigarette stains on china. Use the same treatment for a teapot, or if heavily stained put in a handful of washing soda and fill up with boiling water. Leave to stand until cool, and this will remove the tannin.

When washing up greasy dishes a useful tip is to add a little vinegar to the water

(2 tablespoons per bowl) – it leaves dishes sparkling clean. You can also use lemon juice as a rinse-aid in the rinsing water.

If you have a porcelain sink which needs cleaning, put layers of kitchen paper over the bottom and saturate with undiluted vinegar. Leave for 5-10 minutes, then remove the paper and rub clean. The even contact of the vinegar, plus the length of time it is left in the soaked paper, cleans up the discoloration and brings up the whiteness of the porcelain. For a stainless steel sink, use a damp cloth dipped in white vinegar to remove water spots. Shine by rubbing with soda water.

To keep the sink in good condition, put a cupful of washing soda down the plughole once a week, and wash it down with a kettleful of boiling water to remove any blockages and keep it clean. For limescale around the plughole, rub the deposit hard with the cut side of half a lemon: the acidity dissolves it away. If you get limescale in the kettle, an old-fashioned remedy is to put a marble in the kettle to prevent furring. My method is to cover the element with equal parts of vinegar and water, bring to the boil and leave to stand overnight. Then I rinse it out thoroughly, boil a kettleful and throw away the water before making the next cup of tea.

Flies

If you are plagued by flies in the kitchen, beer or treacle in a saucer or smeared on to sheets of paper, will attract and kill them. If you are eating out of doors, put down a saucer of jam a little distance away – it acts as the perfect decoy for both flies and wasps. Pyrethum powder (from *Pyrethrum cenerariaefolium*) is an environmentally safe fly-repellent. Scatter it around the windowsills or put it on a plate.

Friends who live in a wonderful house in Pennsylvania surrounded by woodland use the leaves of black walnut (*Juglans nigra*) to keep ants and flies from the house. Growing rue outside the kitchen window also repels flies.

Natural Fragrances for the Home

My mother had a keen eye for the elegant and extended her skills to home-made aromatics. I used to help her dry petals and herbs, and loved the days spent mixing the fragrances to make what seemed like magical combinations to scent the house. These are some of the recipes we made together.

Pomanders

These were traditionally threaded on a cord and carried to ward off infection or to mask the evil smells of the street. Sometimes carried in a perforated box of ivory, silver or even gold, they were worn as a fashion accessory.

Pomanders are a lovely way to scent a room, or to perfume a wardrobe, and also to keep moths off in cupboards where you store clothes and fabrics.

1 orange
lots of good quality cloves,
strong and with the heads intact

Stick the orange full of cloves, leaving a space between each one since the orange will shrink. Use a fine knitting needle to make the holes.

Roll the pomander in a mixture of half orris root (*Iris germanica*) and half cinnamon, rubbing it in well. Place in an airing cupboard or warm dry place for 2 weeks, then tie in a ribbon and hang up.

Sweet bags

My mother used to perfume the linen cupboard with these bags, which also keep out moths. You can also hang them over a chair, or loop on to clothes hangers. Use any combination of flowers (see Pot Pourri, below), plus a few drops of essential oil. Make up small bags with muslin or fine linen, attaching a length of ribbon to hang them by.

You can use any of the herbs and flowers suggested for pot pourri, my mother's favourite was dried lemon verbena leaves. Plain lavender bags are hard to beat, too. I make them with little squares of wild silk and tie them with ribbons. They keep their scent for a year. Once you have stripped the stalks, pack these into old stockings and use to scent the airing or linen cupboard.

Flower pot pourri

Bowls of pot pourri add elegance as well as fragrance to a room. You can use scented petals, leaves, flowers and herbs: orange blossom, lemon verbena, honeysuckle, lily of the valley, stocks, lavender, clove pinks, rose petals, sweet geranium, bergamot, violets, jasmine, lemon peel, rosemary and bay leaves, are all excellent.

Dry them on newspaper or muslin in a warm place such as the airing cupboard until they are brittle – about a week to ten days. Put them into a bowl between layers of fixative (use orris root or benzoin powder, 25g/1oz to 1.2 litres/2 pints flowers.) You can also add some ground spices – nutmeg, mace, cloves and cinnamon for example. Then add some whole spices, according to taste (cloves, cinnamon, mace, cumin, allspice). Finally drop in your chosen essential oils.

Turn once or twice a week. The mixture will last from 1-2 years.

Herb pot pourri

Use the dried leaves of peppermint, sweet cicely, sage, basil, rosemary, angelica, lemon thyme, lemon balm. red bergamot, lovage, tarragon, marjoram, rose geranium.

Add ground coriander and nutmeg for a highly aromatic mixture; proceed as above.

Incense

Not really incense but it fills the room with a memorable and exotic scent – flowery and spicy with all the mystery of the East. Stunning.

> *12g (½oz) each dried lavender flowers, rose petals and lemon verbena*
> *12g (½oz) each whole cloves and stick cinnamon, pounded in a mortar*
> *25g (1oz) orris root powder*
> *12g (½oz) gum benzoin*
> *8-10 drops each essential oils of sweet orange, clove, bergamot and rose*

Combine the dry ingredients and mix well. Sprinkle the oils over, and mix again. Store in a dark place for 2 weeks, covered, for the scents to combine. Then place in a metal container on top of a radiator and as it heats gently it will perfume the room.

Herb cushions

Hop pillows are famous for helping insomniacs – King George III couldn't sleep without one. Lavender is excellent too, and rosemary, they say, keeps bad dreams away. You can also use peppermint, sage, lemon balm plus a choice from dill, marjoram, thyme, lemon thyme, tarragon, woodruff, rose geranium, angelica, rosemary, lemon verbena or bergamot.

Dry the leaves as above. Make small pillows (20 cm/8 inches square) using a porous natural fabric such as fine linen or cotton.

A small home-made pillow filled with hop flowers induces deep sleep.

Sweet waters

Distilled flower waters may be used in cosmetic care, for fragrance around the home and in fingerbowls at table, for dipping fingers into between courses. Lavender water, rose water and witch hazel are readily available from chemists and deserve a place in the bathroom cupboard. But some sweet waters are also easy to make at home.

Orange flower water

This was esteemed by Marie Antoinette, who felt it lightened her sallow skin. It is also useful for neutralizing unpleasant smells and as a general household fragrance.

> *1 heaped tablespoon dried orange blossoms, available from herbalists and good apothecaries*
> *90 ml (3 fl oz) boiling water*

Place the blossom in a small bowl and pour on the water. Cover and leave for 15 minutes. Strain off the water, pressing the flowers well. Bottle, and keep in the fridge. Add a little vodka to make it keep longer.

Lavender water

This recipe comes from a Commonplace Book dated 1813.

> *1.2 litres(2 pints) pure alcohol*   *1½ teaspoons essence of ambergris*
> *1 tablespoon oil of lavender*   *5-6 drops musk*
> *1 tablespoon essence of bergamot*

Put all the ingredients into a bottle and shake well. Store for 3 months before use.

A simpler version is to mix 30 ml (1 fl oz) oil of lavender with 900 ml (1½ pints) pure alcohol. Shake well.

Flower waters can be used in any room to freshen the air. They also make great natural skin toners.

BEDROOM

You could say that the bedroom is the most important room in the house: we probably spend more time there than in any other single room. Feng Shui calculates the direction that the bed should face according to the year of your birth, whereas Muslims never lie in a bed with the feet pointing towards Mecca, always the head. An English grandmother told me that she had always been told to place the head of the bed to the north and the foot to the south.

In Feng Shui the shape and element of the headboard can make a significant difference to your energy: rounded metal is good for people engaged in paperwork, rectangular wood for professionals, and oval or wavy shapes for artists and musicians. Don't have too many mirrors in the bedroom – if any – because they attract so much energy into the room that you may have trouble sleeping.

In illness the bedroom becomes a particular focus. Put plants or cut flowers next to the sickbed in order to produce more oxygen during the day, and remove them at night when they put out carbon dioxide. Place a bowl of water on the radiator to relieve a dry cough at night, adding some eucalyptus oil if you like. For a really good night's sleep, sew some lavender buds into your pillow, as lavender is a highly effective sedative. Traditional lore suggests putting a wine cork into the bottom of the bed if you get night cramps; some say a pin magnet does the trick.

Stains on the mattress

Moisten a tablespoon of powdered starch with a little washing-up liquid and apply to the stain. Leave to dry, then brush off with a stiff brush. Alternatively, wearing rubber gloves, sprinkle a damp cloth with a few drops of ammonia and rub off the stain.

Feng Shui recommends an uncluttered bedroom to facilitate the flow of energy.

Cupboards and chests of drawers

My American grandmother left me a chest of drawers made from cedar wood, which is a natural moth deterrent, and I still use it. Line the drawers with fresh paper, and add dried citrus peel or scented bags (see page 19) to keep them smelling fresh and fragrant. This is also a moth-deterrent. Put unwrapped soap into drawers to scent them

or make some simple sachets. For a lavender sachet, take a handful of lavender buds and place in the middle of a square of muslin. You can also add some dried wormwood, an excellent moth repellent. Gather up the edges, and tie tightly with a satin ribbon.

A Dutch friend described how her grandmother aired musty cupboards and drawers. After removing the contents she hung them up outside on a pleasant day to air. Then she crumpled up newspaper, filled the drawers and cupboards with it and left them slightly open for a few days while the paper and ink absorbed damp and smells. Finally she would wipe them out and if possible leave them outside on a breezy day to air thoroughly.

Storing clothes

The Sultan's clothes from around 1450, kept in the Topkapi Museum in Istanbul, are completely intact and look like new. They are folded in linen and laid flat, kept in the dark, and brought to air once a year. The embroidered silks, brocades, damask with gold and silver thread, and tapestry remain as pristine as they were 500 years ago. We can use this simple technique for storing our own clothes.

A Malaysian friend always puts whole cloves – a moth deterrent – into her coat pockets before storing them away for the summer, and into plastic bags with her woollen jumpers. It keeps them far more fragrant than the horrible smell of mothballs.

Mirrors and the dressing table

To clean mirrors, apply a few drops of methylated spirits on a damp cloth, then buff with a clean soft cloth. Don't use water on a mirror: the water may run down into the frame and damage the silvering.

A teaspoon of borax plus a tablespoon of washing soda in warm water will keep hairbrushes clean and fresh.

Add a bunch of thyme to stored clothes to repel moths.

Soak jewellery in a solution of washing up liquid for a few minutes before cleaning with toothpaste and a fine toothbrush – this according to an American friend's grandmother in Ohio. Rinse again, and dry off with a hairdryer. Buff with a soft cloth to bring up the brilliance. Diamonds love gin: they sparkle after a good soaking and then brushing with a toothbrush in warm water.

To keep pearls clean, wear them next to your skin as often as possible – the natural oils in the skin polish them.

Mirror superstitions

Breaking a mirror means seven years' bad luck. But if you wash the broken bits in the stream, or bury them, you reverse the curse.

Primitive man believed that his reflection was that of his soul, and if anything separated it from his body – by breaking the mirror for example – he would die. Something dreadful would happen if you looked in a mirror where a dead person lies because you will see the reflection of the deceased looking over your shoulder. So a custom arose of veiling the mirror. If you look into a mirror and see no reflection that is the worst of all: death is certain, for the soul has already departed. Napoleon believed these superstitions and during a campaign in Italy he broke the glass over a miniature of Josephine that he carried with him. He could not sleep until the courier returned assuring him that no ill had befallen his beloved.

My Russian friend Olga used to love looking at her distorted reflection in the curves of her grandmother's shiny teapot. Grandmother would take the pot away saying 'Never look at yourself in a mirror at table – it will eat up your beauty!'

Bristle brushes should be washed in a weak solution of washing soda to keep them clean.

BATHROOM

Rub liquid detergent on mirrors to prevent them steaming up. When a natural sponge goes slimy, soak it in 1 tablespoon vinegar to 600 ml (1 pint) water. Clean off hard-water marks on tiles or shower doors with neat white vinegar on a soft cloth. Leave for 20-30 minutes, then rinse off.

Rub stubborn marks in the bath with turpentine or white spirit and rinse with hot washing-up solution. For old stains on baths, use equal quantities of turpentine and linseed oil on a soft cloth. Clean off with hot soapy water and rinse thoroughly after use. Use neat paraffin for the most stubborn stains. Scrub stains from dripping taps with lemon juice, using an old toothbrush dipped in salt. You can also make a paste of borax with white vinegar and brush until it disappears.

To remove limescale on taps, rub vigorously with the cut side of half a lemon. Rinse, and buff dry with a clean soft cloth. To descale tap nozzles, tie a plastic bag filled with vinegar over the nozzle and leave until the scale has dissolved, then rinse. Use an old toothbrush to get rid of the grimy deposits around the base of a tap, using vinegar or lemon juice. To clean chrome taps, rub in a handful of flour, then polish off with a soft cloth. If you have a blocked shower-head, soak it in a bowl of warm vinegar and use a toothbrush or darning needle to clear the holes.

When washing lace curtains, add a spoonful of sugar to the final warm rinse, to keep them crisp. If they become discoloured, soak them in cold tea to dye them a creamy-beige. After washing, hang them while still damp so that they don't shrink – pull them gently into shape.

To neutralize smells in the toilet, strike a match. The smell of the sulphur predominates and the flame burns away foul-smelling gases. Alternatively, sprinkle in a sweet water such as orange flower water or lavender water (see page 23).

Liquid detergent, lemon juice and vinegar will cope with most bathroom stains.

31

WASTE NOT, WANT NOT

Leftover wallpaper

Use this to line kitchen shelves and chests of drawers. For the larder shelf, cut 4 or 6 layers to size, and remove a layer regularly as it become dirty, so that your storeroom surfaces are always clean.

Keep leftovers to patch any damaged wall areas: cut out a matching piece slightly larger than the area you need to replace, and if you leave the edge slightly irregular

the patch will be less noticeable. Glue to the spot, matching the pattern carefully and using a roller to flatten the edges.

Good housekeeping

You can increase the shelf-life of a sponge-mop considerably by storing the sponge end with a plastic bag tied around it to stop it drying out and warping. You can save on detergent when you are washing by adding a tablespoon of bicarbonate of soda to the wash. It also softens the water.

'A stitch in time' can repair worn fabric and avoid expensive replacements.

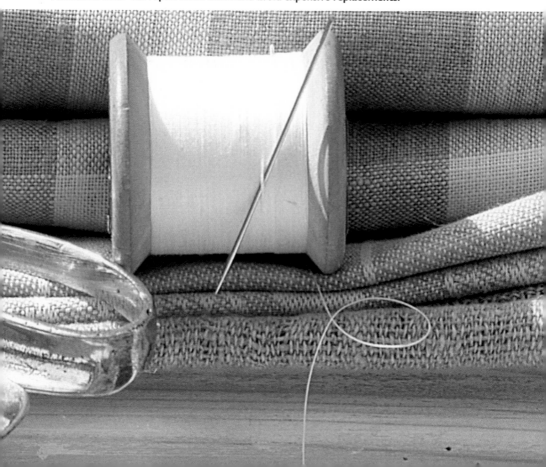

Soften dried-out shoe polish with a little turpentine to give it a new lease of life. To revive an old sponge, an old sock and an old broom handle, attach the sponge to the broom handle and cover with the sock. Use this interesting piece of equipment for cleaning behind your radiators. Change the sock when it gets dirty.

Energy-saving tips

Re-use foil: simply wipe clean with a damp cloth on a flat surface to 'iron' it and prolong its shelf-life; use it to save energy in the following ways:

Place foil inside a grill pan to reflect heat: not only is this an economy, but it is also useful in that you throw away the foil after use rather than having to scrub grease and other deposits off the pan. You can also economize on heat by placing a sheet of foil under the electric hob: this reflects heat back and makes it far easier to keep the stove clean because foil wipes clean easily, burnt objects don't stick, and when it is heavily soiled, you simply throw it away and replace.

Place a sheet of foil under the ironing-board cover to reflect heat into garments.

Old toothbrushes

These are incredibly useful for a variety of jobs: cleaning jewellery (see page 28), scrubbing limescale and deposits off taps (see page 31), cleaning grouting (dipped in a solution of bleach) and polishing intricate woodwork or metal work. They get into otherwise inaccessible mouldings on grates, and into the crannies of complicated kitchen equipment.

Plastic containers

Keep plastic containers (e.g. margarine, yogurt or cottage cheese tubs) to use for freezing food. I put soup into large yogurt containers which conveniently contain one serving. You can also use them as receptacles for cleaning paintbrushes and/or mixing paint.

Save your plastic shopping bags and use them as bin liners. Re-use plastic freezer-bags until they are worn out.

Linen

Turn old tablecloths into a set of napkins. Make pillowcases from sheets which have worn out in the centre but which are still good around the outsides. Use the unworn-out parts of flannelette sheeting for children's nighties.

Give sheets a new lease of life by cutting the sheet lengthwise through the centre where it has worn out, or where it tears, and turn the sides to the middle: sew the outer edges together and make a small neat French seam for strength and smoothness. Hem the outer edges. Make single sheets from double sheets, and keep worn out sheets to use as covers for when you are painting the house, or cut them up and use as polishing cloths.

Always buy recycled paper – it is both elegant and eco-friendly.

CLEANING

Cleanliness is next to godliness, or so it is said in more than one culture. 'Let it be observed, that slovenliness is no part of religion,' preached John Wesley in the 18th century, and Feng Shui has it that clutter, and by implication dirt, blocks the free flow of energy through the home.

Certainly a newly spring-cleaned house is a pleasure, it imparts a sense of the new, of vitality and freshness. Before the days of chemical cleaners our grandmothers used common household or kitchen ingredients to achieve this pristine sparkle: lemons, vinegar, bicarbonate of soda and salt all played a major role, along with the tougher elements of ammonia, methylated spirits, turpentine and white spirit. Borax, glycerine and washing soda have been all but forgotten by the modern housewife, but they are wonderfully effective cleaning agents.

Protect your hands by wearing rubber gloves when using all these strong substances; you'll avoid 'hands like bears' backs' so aptly described by a friend's mother who remembers the days of doing all the family washing by hand. 'What's worth doing is worth doing well' was the adage she repeated often to her daughter. The following tips have been gleaned from people living all over the world, in Singapore, Zimbabwe, Canada and the USA, New Zealand, Iceland and various parts of Europe.

Dusting

The maid of a friend in Singapore always used two dusters while she was cleaning, one in each hand, saying that she would get round in half the time. A good general tip is to soak a new duster in equal parts paraffin and vinegar. Store in a screw-top jar until ready to use, and it will lift out dirt.

Vitality and freshness are integral parts of the natural home.

Polished furniture

Use turpentine, an all-purpose solvent, to remove ring marks, rubbing along the grain. A friend from New Zealand told me that to remove a watermark on polished furniture you should mix a few flicks of cigarette ash with olive oil, rub it in and leave for 30 minutes. Buff with a soft cloth. A mixture of salt and vegetable oil, left on for an hour, also helps remove marks from polished wood. Remove after 30 minutes, then rub with a soft cloth.

To revive dull polish on wooden furniture, mix 2 tablespoons each of turpentine, white vinegar and methylated spirits, which shifts sticky substances, and 1 tablespoon linseed oil, which feeds and protects wood. Shake well, and apply with a soft cloth. For dirty woodwork, mix one part turpentine with one part vinegar and enough powdered starch to make a paste. Put on to a soft cloth and rub into the grime. Buff with a soft cloth.

Rub linseed oil into lustreless oak to make it shine, and when dusting intricately carved wood use a paintbrush or toothbrush. Remove sticky marks on wood with a little vinegar and water, then apply beeswax, the most nourishing of wax polishes.

Home made beeswax polish

This works beautifully and is far cheaper than buying it ready-made.

> *75g (3oz) beeswax*
> *150ml (5fl oz) turpentine*
> *Essential oil of lavender (optional)*

Put the beeswax into a bowl and set it over boiling water until the wax melts. Then add the turpentine and stir thoroughly. Pour into a jar, add a few drops of essential oil of lavender if you wish, and allow to cool.

Making beeswax polish at home is easy, satisfying and effective.

Linseed oil will keep wood surfaces healthy and shiny.

Other surfaces

Marble is porous, so treat stains as soon as possible. For wine, coffee or tea stains, use a solution of 1 part white vinegar to 4 parts water. Wipe off at once. Or apply fresh lemon juice to bleach out the stain. You can remove marks on wallpaper by rubbing with a scrunched up piece of white bread, which also works on hessian.

For grease marks on wallpaper, apply a warm iron over brown paper to absorb the grease. Repeat with clean bits of paper until it disappears. For rust on metal furniture, simply use a stiff wire brush. To revive dull ebony, rub in petroleum jelly, leave to soak in for 30 minutes, then rub off with a soft cloth.

To clean the phone, radios, clock faces and computer keys, use methylated spirits on cotton wool, and penetrate the inaccessible bits with a cotton-wool bud also soaked in it. Two tablespoons methylated spirits and 2 tablespoons water mixed together will clean dirty piano keys: apply on cotton wool, well squeezed out. Be careful with methylated spirits because they are flammable, although they're very useful for removing felt-tip ink and sticky labels.

To clean paintwork, mix 1 tablespoon turpentine, 1 tablespoon milk and 1 tablespoon washing-up liquid with 1.2 litres (2 pints) hot water. Apply with a soft cloth. For scuff marks on vinyl, use an eraser; white spirit or turpentine will also do the job.

Natural leather polish for upholstery

Boil up 300 ml (½ pint) linseed oil, cool and add 300 ml (½ pint) vinegar. Apply with a cloth and then buff to a polish.

Cleaning bamboo furniture

From a friend in Germany:

> *1 tablespoon salt*
> *300ml (1pint) water*
> *a little lemon juice (or a mixture of warm water and washing soda)*

Apply this mixture with a soft brush into the crevices, and wipe dry with an old piece of velvet soaked in linseed oil. Leave the coating of oil on for an hour or 2, then polish off with a soft cloth.

In Singapore, they spray cane and bamboo furniture with water from a plant spray from time to time, to keep it supple.

WASHING

The smell and feel of freshly laundered linen is surely one of life's great pleasures. In the old days a starch was made from the roots of bluebells and arum lilies, and the crushed leaves of soapwort (*Saponaria officinalis*) produced a home-made soap which worked up a good lather. They still do. The presence in the leaves of saponin loosens dirt particles and produces a light lubricating froth which has been used by specialists in modern times to clean fragile antique fabrics.

Recent rust stains on linen can be removed with cream of tartar mixed to a paste with a little water, spread over the affected area, left to dry and then brushed off. You can also try dabbing on lemon juice, covering with salt and leaving to dry for an hour in the sun if possible. Rinse off, then wash. From Singapore: soluble aspirin solution will dissolve underarm sweat stains.

If linen gets marked, dip the stain in buttermilk and dry in the sun, then wash in cold water and dry. For iron moulds and mildew, wet the affected part of the cloth and rub with the cut surface of a lemon. My Indian friend uses lime juice to remove ink and other stains from clothes. Beetroot stains are pernicious: rinse immediately under cold running water, then soak in a borax solution. Borax is a strong detergent which breaks down grease and softens water at the same time. Wash woollen jumpers and wool jersey outfits inside-out, to prevent matting of the pile, and add a tablespoon vinegar to the final rinse to revive colours.

Rinsing

Add 1 tablespoon white vinegar – one of the most versatile of home cleaners – to a bowl of rinse water in hand-washing to remove all traces of soap. A teaspoon of Epsom salts added to the last rinse keeps colours bright. Soak well-used flannels (face-

The fragrance and feel of clean linen is one of the great luxuries of life.

cloths) in 1 tablespoon vinegar or lemon juice to 600 ml (1 pint) water before machine washing, to remove all traces of soap. Soak clothes in cold water prior to washing, to loosen dirt. To keep colours bright, soak clothes in cold salty water before their first wash.

Special treatments

When black garments lose their blackness, soak them in water with a little white vinegar, or add water softener to the wash, to remove the build-up of soap that has caused the colour to change. To revitalize black silk, a woman in the village who had worked 'below stairs' in the local Manor House told me, boil and mash ivy leaves until the water is dark, and it acts as a reconditioning dye.

A friend who is one of the few women I know who loves housework, and whose home always smells of fresh laundry, gave me these tips:

A little methylated spirits added to the rinsing water preserves the sheen of **silk**. Add 2 lumps of sugar to the rinse water to give it body, plus a little lanolin to protect and restore it.

Sprinkle **lace** with powdered magnesia and leave for a few days before shaking it out – this works like a dry shampoo, the powder absorbing the dirt.

To raise the surface of **velvet**, put a wet cloth over a hot iron and hold the velvet over the steam. Brush against the pile with a soft brush and it rises beautifully.

Cleaning the iron

Clean the base of the iron (unplugged) with toothpaste applied with a soft cloth (unless it is non-stick, in which case you sponge it with a washing-up solution, or use methylated spirits).

Simple, natural treatments will keep many delicate fabrics fresh and vibrant.

Pets in the house

A young puppy can cause havoc with your housework until it is house-trained. Neutralize urine smells on the carpets by making a solution of 1 part vinegar to 5 parts water. Put it into a plant-spray bottle to help remove the smell and deter the animal at the same time. Blot the area with ammonia solution (wearing rubber gloves) to act as a further deterrent. Soda water is a useful instant remedy, too.

A chinese woman let me into her secret of deterring cats, she uses citrus fruit peels – they hate the smell!

Wipe oil of cloves on furniture legs to prevent a new puppy from chewing them – they dislike both the smell and the taste.

For pet hairs on furniture, wrap sticky tape around your fingers, sticky side out, and rub your hand over the upholstery to pick up the hairs.

Carpets

For a 'dry shampoo', sprinkle bicarbonate of soda liberally on to the carpet. It neutralizes acid stains and counteracts smells. Leave for 20-30 minutes, then vacuum off. It picks up the dirt beautifully, discourages pests and leaves the carpet smelling fresh.

Shoe-polish stains can be removed by applying white spirit, a versatile solvent. Allow to dry, then dab out any remaining dye with methylated spirits. Dampen a cloth with turpentine and rub away grease spots, then rub softly with a clean cloth to remove traces of the turpentine. Weak vinegar solution is also effective for grease and dirt on carpets. If you find dye stains on the carpet, add a few drops of ammonia to some methylated spirits in a small dish and apply on a cotton pad until the dye vanishes.

If you find cigarette burns on a carpet, rub them with the edge of a silver coin. For beer stains, use a soda syphon, blot well and clean with bicarbonate of soda (see above). If the beer stains are old, use methylated spirits. Tea and black coffee also respond to the soda-syphon treatment; after spraying, sponge with borax solution.

To retrieve tiny objects such as gemstones or contact lenses which become lost in carpet pile, fit a stocking over the nozzle of the vacuum cleaner and it will be sucked into the fabric.

Windows and glass

'The better the day the better the deed,' my neighbour remarked as I was cleaning my cottage windows one sunny morning. Making the glass clear and sparkling brings more light into the rooms, and leaving the windows open for an hour or two afterwards thoroughly airs the house.

For grimy windows, rub first with the cut side of an onion. Then make a solution of water and vinegar and put into a spray bottle. It cuts through grease and brings up a good shine. Wipe newly washed windows dry with crumpled newspaper – the ink gives a good shine. Use horizontal strokes on one side of the glass, vertical on the other, so that you can easily tell on which side there are any smear marks.

For picture glass, glass-fronted dressers and bookcases, or any glass with flyspecks, clean with the cut side of an onion. My old cleaning lady's granny's recipe was to boil up 2-3 onions and use the water to wipe picture frames, glass and windows which flies mark so much during the summer. You can also clean up an oil painting with a cut onion.

A cut onion is useful for cleaning fly specks from glass.

47

Glasses

Add lemon juice to the rinsing water to bring up a shine. For cloudy decanters and vases, mix a handful of salt or crushed eggshell with white vinegar and place inside, then fill with washing-up liquid. Shake well and leave for several hours. Rinse thoroughly. Alternatively, use a solution of white vinegar and water.

Fill cloudy glasses with water and add 1 teaspoon ammonia to each one. Leave overnight and wash clean in hot water. For dull glass, make a paste with baking powder and water and rub it in. Wash off and polish with a soft cloth.

For crystal vases or decanters, put 2 teaspoons of ammonia in the container and fill with water. Leave for several hours, then wash out thoroughly.

Add lemon juice to the rinsing water to make glasses really gleam.

STAINS

The golden rule with stains is to treat them as soon as possible. Laundry borax is excellent, and glycerine helps remove old stains. Glycerine mixed into egg white in equal proportions gets old grass stains out of whites. The world's most universal and natural stain remover is the cut side of half a lemon – the acid is a bleaching agent which takes out unwanted marks and aromas.

Stains on clothes and upholstery

Blood: soak the fabric in cold water.

Chocolate: sprinkle with borax and soak in cold water before washing.

Coffee: rub fresh stains with glycerine and rinse out with warm water.

Egg: soak clothes in cold salty water before washing. Sponge furniture with cold salty water.

Fruit juice: soak in milk for an hour before washing. This also works for cola stains.

Egg: stains cutlery black: wipe off deposits and rub the stains with salt applied on a damp cloth.

Grease: A friend told me she smothered her husband's new silk tie in talc after it became heavily stained with cooking grease. When she brushed it off the next day, the staining had disappeared. Rub suede with glycerine to remove grease; and an emery board will restore shiny patches to their original texture.

Hair oil on a headboard: rub with white spirit.

Ink stains on carpets: A woman now in her nineties who lived in Rhodesia during the early days of her marriage in the 1930s, remembers ink being spilled on a pale pink carpet, and the dog proceeding to trot through it. Black South African servants put milk on the stains and they disappeared without trace.

You can also rub the stain with the cut side of half a tomato, and rinse out well. Scrub ink stains on the hands with a nailbrush dipped in vinegar and salt. Lemon juice

works on this and other dyes left on the hands. For ink stains on wood, dab with neat vinegar on a cotton-wool bud and blot with paper towels. When the stain has cleared, apply wax polish.

Mildew: soak in bleach solution or vinegar before washing and hanging in the sun to dry.

Milk: soak in cold water, then sandwich between kitchen paper and iron out remaining grease.

Tar: scrape off as much as possible, then treat with eucalyptus oil soaked into a white cloth.

Tea stains on upholstery: sponge with a laundry borax solution.

Wine: Sprinkle salt on to a red wine stain on the carpet, and leave to absorb, then brush off. Repeat as necessary. Or pour some white wine over it immediately. Blot well, sponge with clean water and pat dry with kitchen paper. Or use a glycerine solution. On clothes, rinse in warm water, then soak in borax solution (1 tablespoon borax to 600ml/1 pint water) before washing. Old stains may respond to a little methylated spirits on a sponge.

Silver and other metals

During the years that we lived in a Cambridge college my mother ran the Master's Lodge with the help of a wonderful couple from St Helena. Here are some of the tips she picked up from them:

Silver: when tarnished, dissolve a handful of washing soda in an aluminium pan, soak the silver in it and remove as soon as tarnish has disappeared. Rinse and polish. Or use a paste of fine salt and lemon juice. Brighten up silver quickly with a drop of white spirit on a soft cloth.

Pewter: mix wood ash to a paste with a little water and rub it in for a dull sheen. Or rub with cabbage leaves. Alternatively immerse in leftover egg-boiling water. Remove grease marks with a little methylated spirits.

Brass: clean off heavy tarnish with solution of vinegar and salt (1 tablespoon to 600 ml/1 pint), or washing soda. Clean up with lemon dipped in salt, and rub vigorously. Then wash with warm water and ammonia solution (1 tablespoon ammonia to 600ml/1 pint water. Dry and buff to a polish.

Copper: if copper turns green remove the verdigris with a solution of ammonia (see above) using rubber gloves.

Lead: scrub with turpentine or white spirit. If heavily stained, soak 5 minutes in solution of 1 part white vinegar to 9 parts water, with a little bicarbonate of soda added.

Brighten up silver quickly with a drop of white spirit on a soft cloth. Keep a cloth especially for this purpose.

FIREPLACES

Where glowing embers through the room
Teach light to counterfeit a gloom,
Far from all resort of mirth,
Save the cricket on the hearth.

John Milton: *L'Allegro (1632)*

There is a brick jutting out near the top of the chimney in my 300-year-old thatched cottage, and I am told this was called the witch's seat, provided for her so that she would not come down any further. The inglenook has a small cavity in the wall which was used to store the household salt, to keep it dry. Witches hate salt, so I have double protection. One elderly builder told me people used to put salt-glazed bricks into the chimney to keep them away. Be that as it may, an open fireplace is the heart of the house, a place to gather and gaze into the flames to talk and listen to stories and to roast chestnuts. A woman now in her eighties, who used to work as a maid in a stately home in Oxfordshire, was told that the fireplace must be kept spotlessly clean because it was the 'altar of the house'.

Firewood

My German friend Inge was told by her grandfather never to burn elder wood in the house: it was very unlucky because the wood spits and could cause a fire. and anyway it brings the Devil down the chimney. Ash is the best wood – it burns hot and long, and doesn't spit. Pine is dangerous because it sends out showers of sparks so never be tempted to burn up bits of old pine furniture… Cut your wood in the summer and let it 'season' or dry out – wood should not be burned while the sap is running – all it does is hiss at you from the grate. Also, well-seasoned wood is less likely to spark. Keep

Keep logs under cover – they take ages to dry if they are caught in the rain!

A log fire burning in the hearth is the heart of the home.

your wood supply under cover to prevent rain and snow falling on it. If you don't have a wood shed, stack it under a sheet of plastic, allowing air to circulate from the sides.

If you have a large fireplace and need a lot of kindling to start the fire, tie it in a bundle with a twist of pliant twig, such as willow (not string, which burns immediately) – so that the heart of the fire does not collapse. To add fragrance to the fire, throw citrus peel on to it, or pine cones which are beautifully aromatic. If you burn hickory wood it will fill the house with its aroma, and apple wood smells fabulous. You can make good use of wood ash: put ashes on the driveway to make a hard core – gradually it packs down. Or put it on to the garden or the compost heap.

Home-made firelighters

Soak some old newspapers in a bucket of water. When reduced to pulp take handfuls – wearing rubber gloves to protect you from the newsprint – and squeeze into tight balls. Leave to dry out completely and use as firelighters. Straight newspaper is dangerous because it burns so fast and may set fire to the chimney.

Soot marks

Salt helps shift soot marks off the carpets – just sprinkle it over and brush clean. Talcum powder is good too. For soot marks on brickwork surrounding the fire, use a stiff bristle – or even wire – brush dipped in a warm water-vinegar solution, or rub with a another piece of brick. Thick residues of soot may have to be chiselled off. Use neat vinegar for scorch marks. On stonework, use washing-up liquid solution, and add a bit of bleach if necessary.

Cleaning the chimney

An old-fashioned way of sweeping the chimney over a wood fire was to drop one end of rope with a big bunch of holly leaves tied halfway along it, big enough to thoroughly scrape the edges, down the chimney. You have one person at each and work up and down until the chimney is cleaned of excess soot.

Toasting goodies by the fireside

Get yourself a toasting fork and make toast, holding the bread at a judicious distance from the flame so as not to burn it. Likewise with marshmallows, just get them hot enough and near enough to the flame to give them a crust all over the outside, then remove, cool a little and you will find the inside gooey. You can even try an impromptu 'fondue', putting 2cm/¾inch cubes of cheese on to the toasting fork, turning them in the flame until they begin to melt. This takes practice: it is easy to overcook and lose the whole thing with a hiss as it disappears into the flames. When you succeed, however, the smoky flavour and the melting texture are fabulous. But beware of putting anything cooked like this straight into your mouth – you could be horribly burned by the hot metal of the fork. Always remove the hot article on to a plate first, to cool a little before you eat it.

If you have a big wood fire with a heap of hot ash underneath, bake potatoes there by smothering them and leaving them to cook in the hot ashes for about an hour. Best of all on winter nights are roasted chestnuts: wait until the fire dies down, slit the tops of the chestnuts, which otherwise will explode violently, and put them into the hot embers. Leave for 5-7 minutes before picking out carefully with tongs. Alternatively, use a chestnut roaster, an iron holder with holes in, on a long handle. Hold it over the fire for 5-7 minutes, then allow to cool before you peel them.

Toasting marshmallows by the fire – one of the great joys of a cold winter evening.

CANDLES

Candles were invented in the ancient world, as evidenced by Egyptian and Cretan candlesticks dating back to 3000BC. There is a legend that King Alfred the Great (849-899) used candles to measure the passing of time: placed in a lantern to protect them from draughts, each one would burn for four hours. By 1272, according to a tax list, there were 71 chandlers or candlemakers working in Paris.

The soft light of a candle brings beauty to a room and is flattering to the skin, but its romantic connotations are not without risks: 'Choose neither women nor linen by candlelight,' says country wisdom. Nowadays there are floating candles, scented candles, and candles of many colours and shapes for creating atmosphere within the home. Modern candles are a composite of paraffin and stearic acid, sometimes with beeswax or bayberry wax added.

Candles have been used for centuries in religious and spiritual ceremonies, and in rituals all over the world. The Roman Catholic Church used to stipulate that candles were 100% pure beeswax, but now the measure is down to only 25%. There was a tenth-century Welsh law that stated a Mass could be said only when bees were present – in the form of beeswax candles. Bees are holy because they swarmed out of Paradise in disgust at the Fall of Man.

The obvious analogy of lighting the darkness made candles symbols for purity and enlightenment:

I shall light a candle of understanding in thine heart, which shall not be put out.
Esdras 8.25

If you put a candle in the freezer for a few hours, it will burn for longer.

Practical tips

Place new candles in the freezer for a few hours to make them burn longer. Dip a candle end in very hot water to soften it before putting into a candlestick: heating it with a match marks it black. If the holder is loose, wrap the end of the candle in tape.

When removing wax from pewter candlesticks, place them in the freezer for an hour or two, then the wax peels off easily. Use a hairdryer to melt away the rest. On china candlesticks, remove the excess with a blunt knife, then place in the microwave on full power for 1-2 minutes to soften the remaining wax, which you can then rub off

easily. With silver candlesticks, pour hot water over the candlestick to remove the wax. Melt the remainder with a hairdryer.

To clean candlewax off a wood surface, let it harden (speed this up with an ice cube), then ease off with a blunt knife, rub in some polish and buff with soft cloth.

Allow spilt wax on the carpet to harden. Gently scrape off what you can without damaging the pile. Then set the iron to warm and blot the rest of the wax through absorbent kitchen paper and keep changing it until all traces of wax have disappeared. On clothes, treat with methylated spirits which will also absorb colour dye. On wallpaper and furniture, use the paper technique.

The soft light from candles is flattering to the skin.

To make a rush candle

Rushlights were once the most economical
source of lighting for rural homes. Here is an
old-fashioned recipe for making a rush taper (it
would be mounted on to a piece of tree bark
and lit to give a soft light after dark). The great
advantage of rush lights is that they do not drip.

Cut soft rushes (*Juncus effusus* or *J.
conglomeratus*) when they are fully grown but
still green. Cut off both ends, peel the green
skin and hang up to dry.

Melt some grease – mutton is best, or the
grease obtained from boiling marrow bones.
Add beeswax to make it burn extra bright.
Soak the rushes in the grease and take them
out to dry hard. Do this several times until
well coated.

**Beeswax candles burn brightly and
last longer than cheap shop-bought
varieties.**

Superstitions and sayings

Candles have given rise to many common sayings: 'to hold a candle to the devil' is to
assist an evil person. If 'the game is not worth the candle', the enterprise is not worth
the labour or expenditure. 'To burn the candle at both ends' is to keep excessively long
waking hours. To be 'not fit to hold a candle to' means not to be compared with.

It is unlucky to light a candle from the fire on the hearth. The accumulation of wax
dripping to one side of a candle foretells death, because it looks like a shroud. To snuff
a candle accidentally is a portent of a wedding. An actor friend told me that three
candles in the dressing room, or on the stage, bring bad luck.

COMMON SUPERSTITIONS

My neighbour, now in her 80s, remembers how women in the village used to be ruled by superstition. Some have a practical value but many are quite obscure; what is fascinating is that they seem to have universal appeal. All cultures have them, representing a kind of accessible magic to protect us from harm by unseen forces, a magic distinctive to the society in which it originated, but which may also find echoes in another, however distant.

Household

'Touch wood' is said to have come from the days when relics of the True Cross were kept in churches and solemn oaths were sworn on them. The wrought iron S and X shapes on cottage walls have a superstition behind their obvious practical use: they act as lightning conductors as well as wall props, but the S represents the thunderbolt of Jupiter, the X or swastika the hammer of Thor. Acorns used to be hung at the window to protect the house from lightning, and window-blind pulls are still today fashioned as acorns: the sacred nature of the oak, Jupiter's tree, brought into the home.

Never hang a garment on a doorknob, my neighbour told me, because they used to hang a piece of clothing on the outer knob of the door to tell you that someone inside had died. Never open an umbrella in the house, said a man from Minnesota, and my Dutch friend Mineke's mother used to scream at her for doing it. If you drop it make sure it is picked up by someone else. Spilling salt is unlucky: to reverse this you must immediately throw some over your left shoulder. Salt used to be very expensive, and was heavily taxed in Holland. Mineke was told that there would be a row, and that if you dropped butter on the floor it meant you would have a visitor. Breakages always come in threes, according to many.

Everyone knows that horseshoes are lucky, but remember that they should be nailed upwards, and with their own nails. Upside down, all the good luck spills out.

Spiders

Spiders have long been supposed to bring good luck and prosperity:

If you wish to live and thrive
Let the spider run alive.

One legend goes that during the Flight into Egypt Joseph hid the Holy Family in a cave and a spider wove a web across the entrance. Seeing it unbroken, the pursuing soldiers concluded that no one had entered.

A young woman who lived on Tahiti for a while told me that spiders there are sacred because they are thought to be 'shadows of the gods', and to kill one was extremely unlucky.

Cats

A local thatcher told me that his grandfather used to put a dead cat into the thatch as he worked, to protect the house from evil spirits and fire. A Mexican man told me that in Bolivia they put cockerels into the fabric of the house to avert the evil eye.

A 300-year-old mummified cat – buried alive in the brickwork of a fireplace to ward off evil spirits – was found in the Mill Hotel In Sudbury in Suffolk by builders doing renovations. They tossed the gruesome object into the skip. Over the next four years the mill's foundations started to subside, its fabric to crumble, and a major fire broke out. The builder, knowing something about cat superstitions, had not dared throw the cat away, and the manager persuaded him to retrieve it from his yard. It is now restored to pride of place in a glass casement in the hotel entrance. And no further harm has come to the building.

Witches' 'familiars', sacred objects, bringers of good or bad luck – cats have been surrounded by superstition for thousands of years.

FESTIVALS IN THE HOME

The great religious festivals of the world bring families and communities together to perform traditional rituals, often residues of pagan ones, which include, not least importantly, feasting. The bonding effect that these events have make it an important time for the family, in whichever part of the world. For Diwali, India's festival of Light, small earthenware lamps are filled with oil, placed in their temples and houses, and set adrift on rivers and streams. At the Jewish Passover bitter herbs are eaten, symbolising the bitter life of the Hebrews under the Egyptian yoke. Today celery, romaine lettuce, parsley, chicory and horseradish root are served. The Chinese celebrate their New Year with colourful pageantry and feasting, the Mexicans mark their Day of the Dead,

the Druids the Summer Solstice and the Irish St. Patrick's Day. Easter is a major festival in the Christian world, whereas the Japanese celebrate the Buddha's birthday at Kambutsue. And so on and so on: human beings love to celebrate, and no more so than at Christmas and Thanksgiving.

Many people feel that Christmas is over-commercialised. But you can still make your own cards and decorations and wreaths – I shall never forget one beautiful one made by an American friend simply with the evergreen herbs, rosemary, thyme, rue, winter savory and sweet laurel. Certainly your own home-made food, made in the tradition of our mothers and grandmothers, gives Christmas that personal touch and family feel: this tiny selection gives a flavour of the charm of an old-fashioned Christmas.

CHRISTMAS

Frosted holly leaves

This old-fashioned and very pretty notion was given to me by a lady approaching her hundredth birthday, who told me that she remembered her grandmother making them, for decorating the Christmas cake.

sprigs of holly • melted butter • caster sugar

Pick the leaves from their stalks and wipe them clean and dry. Hang up in the airing cupboard to dry for two days. Then dip them into melted butter, dip into caster sugar and put them on to a tray. Return them to the airing cupboard or over the boiler to dry for a further two days.

Christmas cookies

Makes 24

These are the Proustian madeleines of my life. My American mother used to make 'sugar cookies', as she called them, and they are an integral part of childhood, bringing distant memories into focus.

100g (4oz) plain flour
100g (4oz) granulated sugar
100g (4oz) butter
grated zest of half a lemon
2 teaspoons vanilla

Mix the flour with the sugar and rub in the butter until it is like very fine breadcrumbs, then add the lemon zest and vanilla. Knead on a wooden board to a soft dough. If you want them to hold their shape, add a little more flour (a scant 15g/½oz) to make a stiffer dough.

Roll out fairly thinly and cut into rounds or other shapes – either make up your own and do them freehand, or use cutter shapes (stars, trees, angels etc.) If you are going to hang them on the tree, puncture a small hole near the top edge before baking. Bake at 180°C/350°F/gas mark 4 for 8-10 minutes, until a light golden colour. Allow to cool for 3-4 minutes, then lift off carefully and cool on a wire rack.

Cranberry rope

This Christmas decoration was described to me by a woman living in New York City who remembered picking cranberries as a child in the bogs near her home in Massachusetts.

Pick cranberries and clean them. Thread a medium needle with waxed thread and thread the cranberries carefully on to it, making the rope as long as you need. You can also alternate the berries with popcorn to make a red and white rope. The berries dry out over the days and end up like beads, and of course they shrink which makes the rope shorter – so allow for this by making it extra-long. The occupational hazard of this is that your hands get stained red (remove the stain with lemon juice).

This rope looks extremely pretty twisted around the light wires on the tree.

Lamb's wool

Rural traditions are rich in celebratory cups: special brews to mark particular festivals still add vitality and individuality to rural life in many parts of Europe.

Lamb's wool is a country Christmas drink made with baked apples in strong ale, spiced with nutmeg and ginger, and sweetened with raw sugar. It was made in earthenware vessels and was originally dedicated to the angel presiding over fruits and seeds. Some friends of mine in the west country still make it every winter to an original recipe and for them Christmas would not be the same without it.

Per person
2 apples
600ml (1 pint) beer
½ teaspoon ground nutmeg
1 teaspoon ground ginger
100g (4oz) brown sugar

Preheat the oven to 180°C/350 °F/gas mark 4.

Cut the apple into quarters crosswise, put into a metal tray and bake for 30 minutes. Warm the beer gently and add the spices and sugar. Stir until dissolved, about 3-4 minutes, being careful not to overheat. Float the apples on top and the Lamb's wool is ready to serve.

Lamb's wool is a traditional English country drink made with apples, spices and beer.

THANKSGIVING

The North American tradition of Thanksgiving goes back to the autumn of 1621 when Massachusetts Bay Governor William Bradford invited neighbouring Indians to join the Pilgrims for a three day feast in gratitude for the harvest and the blessings of the past year. It caught on. Thanksgiving Day was proclaimed a national holiday by Abraham Lincoln in 1863, and Canada adopted it in 1879. Turkey, cranberry sauce and pumpkin pie are the order of the day.

Stuffed acorn squash with wild rice and mushroom stuffing

A wonderful dish to serve up alongside the turkey and cranberry sauce. Serves 8-10.

1 2.25kg/5lb acorn squash

For the stuffing

100g/4oz wild rice	*50g/2oz cheese, grated*
1 teaspoon salt	*2 teaspoons ground ginger*
25g/1 oz butter	*Salt and pepper*
175g/6oz mushrooms, chopped finely	*100g/4oz brown breadcrumbs*
50g/2oz red onion, chopped finely	*3 tablespoons olive oil*

Preheat the oven to 200°C/400°F/gas mark 6. Put the squash on to a baking sheet and bake for 50-60 minutes, until a sharp knife inserted into the centre goes in easily and all the flesh is soft. Cool, then cut in half horizontally and scrape out the seeds and fibres.

Cook the wild rice for 30 minutes in boiling water, or until tender, adding the salt during the last 5 minutes. Cook the mushrooms and onion in the butter for 4-5 minutes until softened. Mix in the cooked wild rice with the cheese and ginger and season to taste. Preheat the oven to 180°C/350°F/gas mark 4.

Pile the filling into the cavities of the squash. Crisp the breadcrumbs in the olive oil, tossing until coated all over. Sprinkle the squash with the crumbs and bake in the bottom of the oven (to prevent the crumbs burning) for 35-40 minutes.

Old-fashioned cranberry sauce

This recipe was given to me by a grandmother who has been making this sauce since the 1940s. She used to make it with canned cranberries, I used fresh: take your pick.

250g/8oz cranberries, canned, fresh or frozen
300g/10oz mandarin orange sections from a can, with juices
75g/3oz granulated sugar
50g/2oz walnut sections

Simmer the cranberries with the mandarins and their juices, the sugar and the walnuts, until they are mushy – about 5 minutes. Then crush lightly with a potato masher, and it is ready to serve. It is absolutely brilliant, and it freezes well. As you've got enough to do what with all the rest of the food, the simplicity of this labour-saving sauce is a godsend.

Pecan pumpkin pie

A great finale to the feast. This is the best recipe I've ever tasted for pumpkin pie: it will dispel all doubts that non-Americans may have about this delicacy. It is scrumptious, light, mouthwatering, gastronomic. You will find it unforgettable.

1 23cm/9inch flan case lined with 250g/8oz shortcrust pastry
500g/1lb slice of pumpkin, deseeded
150 ml/¼ pint single cream
3 eggs, lightly beaten
175g/6oz brown sugar
2 teaspoons cinnamon
½ teaspoon each allspice, ginger and nutmeg
Pinch of salt
2-3 tablespoons brandy (optional)
50g/2oz pecan halves

Line the pastry with foil, fill with baking beans and bake blind at 170°C/325°F/gas mark 3 for 20 minutes. Remove the foil and leave to cool in the oven.

Wrap the pumpkin in foil and bake at 200°C/400°F/gas mark 6 for 25-30 minutes until tender. Cool, then remove the skin. Blend to a purée in the food processor, and add the cream. Beat the eggs with the sugar, spices and salt until they are thick, and fold in. Flavour with brandy and pour into the prepared pie shell. Decorate the top with the pecan halves.

Bake at 200°C/400°F/gas mark 6 for 40 minutes, or until a knife inserted into the centre comes out clean. Cool on a rack and eat warm, served with thick cream and followed by a cup of the best coffee. Happiness.

Everlasting syllabub

'Bub' is sixteenth-century slang for a bubbling drink, traditionally made by mixing wine and brandy with whipped frothing cream. Sill was a region of Champagne which provided the bubbles. Later, a syllabub became a richer mixture, made with wine or spirits but about four-fifths cream and spooned rather than drunk out of glasses. Then someone discovered that if you reduced the proportion of wine and sugar to cream, it would not separate: this became the basis of the 'Everlasting Syllabub'.

1 23cm/9inch flan case lined with 250g/8oz shortcrust pastry
1 lemon
125ml (4 fl oz) sherry or white wine
2 tablespoons brandy
50g (2oz) caster sugar
300ml (½ pint) crème fraîche
Whole nutmeg
2 egg whites
Small edible rose petals, to decorate
Caster sugar

Pare the lemon rind thinly and put into a bowl with the wine and brandy. Leave for several hours or overnight.

Strain into another bowl. Add the sugar and stir until dissolved. Pour in the *crème fraîche* slowly, beating all the time with a wire whisk. Grate in a little nutmeg and fold in one stiffly whisked egg white. Spoon into small glasses and keep in a cool place (not the fridge) until ready to eat. The syllabub can be made 2-3 days in advance. Decorate just before serving with rose petals dipped in egg white, then frosted with caster sugar.

INDEX